MEATBALLS

TRACY EMM

MEATBALLS

ISBN: 979-8-218-26275-4

Cover design by: Fatima Seehar
Poetry Illustrations by: Rein G.
Poems and Prose Written by: Tracy Emm

To all those who helped shape
who I am today.
I am forever grateful.
I love you always.

CONTENTS

Ancestry

What would it mean to make every woman
who came before you proud
To stand on their stained aprons and
unpublished diaries
To let the world feel the heartbreak they held
like sacred shattered pieces between their ribs
To give voice to the stories they kept muffled
for fear of their own dismantling

Rewind the clock
Let your tiny innocent hands wipe the tears
off your mother's face
Sit by your grandmother's side and give her
the courage to sign the papers
Knock the condemning pointed finger of the
church out of her face
Scream your guttural screams
Let every man who stuffed down their feelings
Awaken to the sound of your roar

Allow the heartache to take you home

Part 1: The Weaving

Meatballs

My favorite memory of my mother
Is watching her make meatballs
As I sat perched on the kitchen countertop
Bare bottom cold on the speckled granite
Feet dangling below me
Waiting patiently to shove my tiny hands
In that large bowl of ground beef and
parmesan
Watching her read back grandmother's recipe
Using her shoulder to push dark red locks out
of her face
So her eyes could follow the sloppy cursive
Like the sloppy red sauce
On my t-shirt
Which will tell its own story
In stubborn stains
With time

Lost

We spent all day in the sunshine and the salt
of the ocean
Constructing castles made of tiny grains of
sand
And watching them get devoured by the
rolling waves of foam

Time to go!
My mother finally called
Grab everything you brought

And so I picked up each colorful sand toy
The mini blue shovel and the shiny red
bucket
And I placed them in their loosely netted bag
Swung it over my shoulder and then went to
grab my shoes
My favorite pair of see-through sparkly jellies
Sandals that felt like squishy heaven on my
toes

But my left shoe was nowhere to be found
I overturned piles of sand and sifted through
toys
Felt my heartbeat quicken with panic

Maybe a wave took it
Mom said
We have to get going now
It will be OK

It's replaceable
But I was devastated

I walked back to the car with a limp
My left foot mourning its once-adorable
home

I hadn't yet learned
That what is taken away from us
Gets replaced by something new
That life is about losing things gracefully
A dance we must learn between holding
on firmly and allowing the sand to move
through our fingertips
That most of what we love can be claimed as
ours only for a precious moment
Before they are carried back out to the sea

Brown Eyed Girl

I watched dad spin mom around
Hold her in his arms and dip her down at
just the right moment
Right before Van hit the *shalalalalala*
He'd stare into her big brown eyes
And sing that song as if he wrote it

.
.
.

Slowly those dances morphed into screaming
matches
Our kitchen now resembling a courtroom
over a dance floor
Their once palpable love fading into a
memory
He was no longer asking for her hands to
hold and her body to twirl
He was begging for forgiveness

But her adoration was turning into
resentment
How many nights she waited for him to come
home
Masquerading her disappointment as apathy
Hiding her tears with fictitious laughs
As she played with sister and me
Pretending not to notice the ticking hands of
the clock

Pig

Mom drove with fury
Her blue minivan skidding around each
corner
Blasting Alanis out of the tiny speakers

She wouldn't tell us where we going
But we recognized the route
Dad had taken us here before

Told us to play at the arcade games
As he chugged a cold beer at the bar
Flirting with a local blonde

But this time we didn't go in
All she needed was to see his car
Sitting callously in the front parking lot
Shiny Tahoe filled with lies

She took out her lipstick
A fiery red
Etched P-I-G across his front windshield

This time he'll know
Her heart is less forgiving
Than his windshield

Suitcase

Your mother doesn't want me here anymore
That was his excuse
Rolled too easily off of his tongue
His reason for packing his life into a suitcase
In front of a six year old
And walking out the door
As if my mother forced him into the bed of
another

What if I had screamed
Fight for us
This family you pretended you wanted
But then realized
Wasn't worth trading in
Long nights at the bar for

Would it have changed his mind
Coming from my innocent mouth

Boobs

I watched you unravel the bandages
Wrapped tightly around your chest
What's that for
I blurted unapologetically
The way only a kid can
Just support
You lied
The way only adults can

You'll later tell me
You sucked the life out of them
I once had great ones

And isn't that so true
Didn't I suck the life out of you
With worry and stress and schedules

If only all things
Were so easily replaced
At the hands of a surgeon
Making a living off of a woman's inability
To see herself perfect as is

.

.

.

.

.

.

Revenge tits
Dad told us
After you came to the door to greet him
When he arrived an hour late
To pick us up for our weekend visit
Your smile wide with satisfaction
Hard nipples piercing through your white
cropped tee
Cutting right through his heart
At the mistake he made
In losing you

Life

My first experience with exclusion
10 and up
Tiny words etched on the side of a board
game box
My astute sister pointed
Look! You can't play with us
Not my rules
You're not big enough

My eight year old self stood silent
Pupils darting across the closed circle
Searching for sympathetic eyes to meet mine
For one of our friends to shout
Let her in! It's fine
But their lips didn't move
So there I stood
Outcasted to the sidelines
Glancing at the game board
Watching the tiny cars
With their little plastic families
Slowly inch along each colored square
Picking up a child or two along the way

I didn't need to play
I learned more about life never touching those
game pieces
Just observing from the sidelines
How righteousness can bleed onto others
Making people feel powerful
When in truth they are cowards

How we try to control our fate
By changing out the cards
Justifying cheating
Because it's what we deserve

How even at the age of ten
Girls envision a perfect life
Of marriage kids and a career
As if this journey were just a series
Of predetermined moves

But what that game taught me most
Was how the cards we're dealt
Like the year we're born
Can determine the outcome of the game
And the rules we play by
Are of our own making

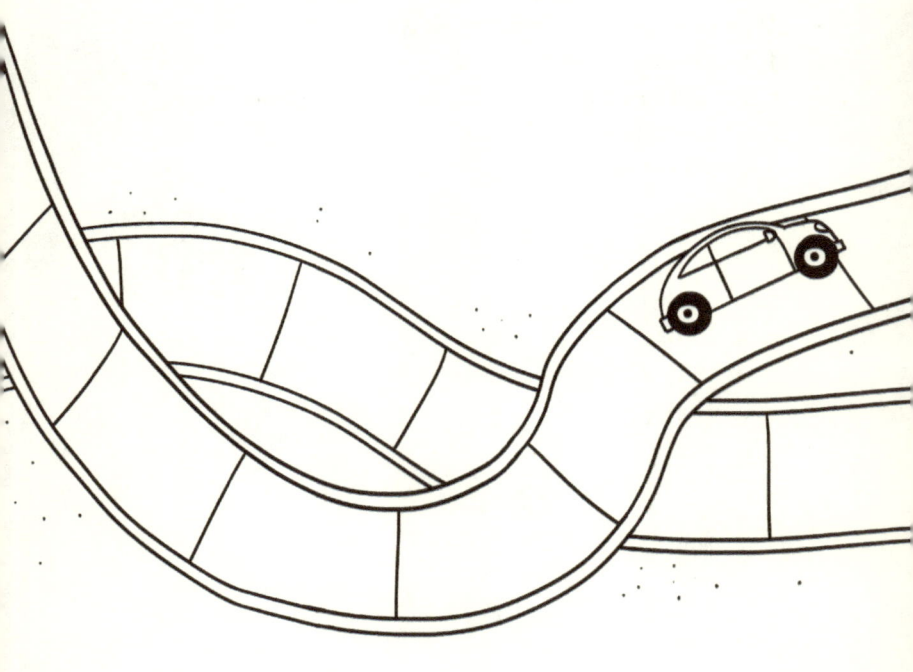

Psycho

Psycho
Psycho
Psycho

Her whispers may have been soft
But they amplified loudly in my head
Each *Pssss* sending chills down my spine

Come on out psycho

I clasped my hands so tightly around my ears
I thought I'd get lost in the sounds of the sea

But her words were too incessant

I looked at the translucent purple clock
Sitting on my whitewashed nightstand
It was barely a quarter past five
Another hour before mom got home

Don't move from the door
She'll pry it open the second your body weight lifts
off of it
And your face will become the cushion for her angry
hand
.
.

.

.

Who started it?
Mom would ask
As we both greeted her in tears
I'd watch my sister lie
Her face stone cold with dishonest conviction

Swallowing my truth with every gulp of
frustration
My stomach becoming a graveyard
For all those tattles I didn't tell

Kite

The kite flew so high it became a second sun
Long streamers glimmering
Every time our star hit its iridescent tail
At just the right angle

Hold here
The wind is moving southbound
Use two hands and make sure to not let go

His fatherly tone deep and concerning
But my little hands
Were too weak
The wind took it
Like it was hungry for a snack
Carried it to the stomach of the marsh
Up and over the highway

I must have cried a good cry
A sound he wasn't used to hearing
And so he did whatever he could
To get that kite back

Ran across the street
Searching in the wetlands
For what would be remnants
Of my fallen star

And for the first time
Since he packed his suitcase
I realized he'd still be there
I saw the word father
In his determined eyes
As he tried desperately
To reclaim what I had lost

His heart strings like kite streamers
A glimpse of shimmer
Waiting to be found

Holes

Think before you speak
You can't take back the words you say
Two phrases my mother echoed to deaf ears
Our pre-teen tongues got a taste of the power
of words
And we couldn't help but indulge in its
decadence
Using its venom to draw tears from our
opponent

I can't remember the exact words that were
exchanged
But they must have stung
Left mom speechless
Which didn't happen often
Coming from the mouth of a New Yorker

I'm sorry
I pleaded
But it meant nothing
She took my sister and me out in the
backyard
Making a dramatic metaphor
Of what words can do
Grabbing a hammer and nail on her way

You see this
Every time you say something hurtful
It's like a nail piercing through the heart

She pounded on the fence
As our faces scrunched and eyes rolled
Watching the nail puncture the weathered
two-by-four

Go ahead
Take it out
Say you're sorry
Apologize

But what's still there
The hole remains
The fence doesn't forget

No words of apology
Can stitch up the hole
That is left behind
When hatred drills its nails
Into our psyche
And into our hearts

Hands

I skated madly around the roller rink
Smooth wheels against a waxed floor
Crashing into the side walls
Unable to slow down
But knowing that red carpeted wall
Would catch me
Just as I wished he would

And soon enough
As the lights dimmed
And the music slowed
I felt his sweaty palm grab mine

Our feet began to match strides
And I got lost in our rhythm
Eyes glued to the wood floor beneath me
Too blushed to meet his

I secretly hoped that love song would last
forever
And we could skate around the rink
Smell of stale popcorn in the air
Until our legs grew weak

How he made my pre-teen heart skip a beat
Like the amateur DJ skipped the latest pop
track
With only the light touch of his fingertips
Wrapped loosely in mine

Stepfather

His eyes were blue
Just like dads
But nothing else the same
Neighbors turned lovers
Turning you back into a teenage girl
Face beaming at the sound of his name

You deserved a man like him
To listen to your heart
To be present and kind
To make you feel strong and worthy
Yet feminine and soft

After being with a man
Who was the center of his own universe
Bill made you his
Orbiting around you
Propping you up
To the throne you belonged on

And he treated us the same
A calming shade of blue
In a house of fiery reds
A simple-minded soul
Amidst minds of tangled webs
The antithesis to our nature
And yet the glue to mend our ragged fence

Birthmark

If I could I'd burn you off myself
I remember thinking
As if the scar that'd be left behind
Wouldn't be worse
Than the state-sized freckle
On the back of my left calf
A site of recognition
For anyone behind me
A stamp of imperfection
A cry to be teased

I dreaded wearing PE shorts
Knowing the boy behind me
Would make mockery of my own skin
There's poop on your leg
He'd screech
As we stood on our white painted dots

But that I can't control
Unlike the shit
Blurting out of your mouth

.

.

.

I am not sure at exactly what age
We learned to play hack sack with our pains
But I am nearly certain that middle school
May be our nation's version of mandatory
service

Pre-algebra taught us how to find x: the
missing insecurity
And English
Every synonym for the word *loathe*
And woodshop
How to better drill nails into hearts

And we all graduated
A bit bruised but with uniforms built of armor

Apartment

Three hundred Newport Street
Two blocks from a dive bar that served free
peanuts
Ten blocks from my college campus
And what felt like hundreds of miles away
From the home I spent eighteen years in

A tiny square of imperfection
In a complex filled with strangers
With walls so thin I could feel a neighbor's
presence
By the way their feet shook the floor above me
I knew every peeve and every joy of the lady
next door
Because I could so clearly hear her sighs and
exhalations
I fell asleep listening to the squeaks of the
washer
That rested on the other side of my wall
Wish wash
Wish wash

I made a refuge
Of that overpriced apartment
A small taste of freedom
A space to come back home
To myself

Butterfly

I don't understand!
You screamed
How could nature be so cruel

To inch along as a worm
Then crawl into darkness
Only to emerge with crippled wings
Unable to fly

But there you were
The mother of all mothers
Inherent nurturer
Savior of all things broken
Be it men or creatures
Abandoned kittens
Baby birds fledged too soon
Our house a welcome invitation
For all things needing mending

But this you could not fix
You kept that flightless butterfly alive
Safely in your terrarium
Bringing him nectar and watching him
heedlessly flap

But what life is that
Butterflies were not meant to crawl
Let nature take its course!
I pleaded

But I knew what that creature represented

You wanted so badly
To rewrite destiny
To save your husband's ailing body
Kept alive in the safety of your nursery

Awaiting his flight home

Gray

Does he fear the darkness
And how it may swallow him whole
The silence a deafening absence
Of a life that once sang

Imprisoned by his mind
As his body slowly collapses
Blue eyes turning gray
Strong arms turning bony

How the days must move so slowly
Time irrelevant
Only the aches of his body
A painful reminder
That he's still here
Watching the sun rise and fall
On an Earth he'll soon leave

Cancer

Most could barely make eye contact
They'd briefly ask how I'm doing
Like it was a box they had to check
Or offer their apologies
As if they stuck the cancer in him themselves
Diverting their gaze
When my eyes began to swell with tears
At the mention of his name
No one wanted to really listen
And I wouldn't dare put the burden on them
But oh
How I wanted to let it all pour out
The pain I felt
The pain I witnessed
As he gasped for air
Breathing tubes stuck up his bloody nostrils
The shame he felt
That I felt as mine
As his weak body draped over my shoulders
Silently walking down the hallway together
Too scared to acknowledge
The end we knew was coming

.

.

The pain I heard in my mother's screams
As she was slowly pried from his dead body
Holding his pale gray hands
And brushing the few thin strands of hair he
had left on his head
As if he could still feel it

He's not there mom
He's not there anymore
It's time to let go

Maybe I should have let her stay there
Let her take in the scent of his flesh a little
longer
Let the realization of his lifeless body sink in
Before she was rushed to sign paperwork
Before his face would only be seen again in
two-dimensions

Everyone's sorry
But life moves on
Doesn't it?

Grief

Sometimes I want to lie in the grass
Feel my body heavy against the Earth
Let the tears I've cried while mourning your
leaving
Water the ground below me
Pouring myself back into it
Bit by bit
Until I'm home again
Until every ounce of me
Gets devoured
By the trees and the bees

Heaven

When you arrived in heaven
Did the angels recognize your sweet soul
And say you were already one of them

Are you traveling to the parts of the world
you thought you'd never see
New Zealand Iceland Australia
Hopping next to kangaroos with your soft
feathered wings

Did your father greet you with the kisses he
withheld during your childhood
And a heart that's now cracked open from
God's love

Do you spend hours watching the sunrise
over the Dakotas
The plains you once called home
Marveling at the way those delicate blades of
grass stand firm in the wind
And shaking your head at all the beauty you
had failed to notice

Does the world look even smaller now that
your angle has changed
Because from down here it shrank in size the
second your big smile departed

to Death:

When death comes knocking on my door
I'll tell him he better move swiftly
I will not watch my body achingly decay
I am no snack to be slowly bitten off one day
at a time as my strength withers
This sweet little body of mine deserves to be
spooned up in one mouthful by his darkness
I'll shout to him
Take me all at once you coward!

But I'll remind him
He's got one hell of a fight to put up
I am not ready to leave
I've got work to do here
Pages that need to be filled with my thoughts
Hearts that need to be mended by my words
       Maybe some broken too
Souls that need to be tickled by the sound of
my laughter
Bodies that need to feel my delicate touch

No I can't go just yet
I've still got children to bear
For I've felt a lover on my breasts
But never the result of our sweet love making
laid across my chest
And that is a feeling I can already tell will
swell my heart so large
He may not even have a job left to do at all

Boobs Pt. 2:

I can't imagine
When you felt that pea size lump
The thoughts that flooded your mind
The memories that returned to you
Of your mother's long battle
The fear that must have struck you
Of a future you were all too familiar with

Your once perfect breasts
On a chest filled with pain
Of the lover you had to bury

Did sorrow and worry
Spill out of your heart
And poison your body with grief

Cut it out!
You insisted

What good are those breasts
Now that the eyes that marveled them
The hands that caressed them
Have left this world

Mother:

How difficult it must have been
To be two parents
Lover and punisher
Savior and confider
Teacher and friend

Striving to make up
For father's lack of presence
Squeezing love from every inch of your heart
Pouring devotion

Attempting to make me feel full

Helping me to see the value
In every woman I encounter
The way we nurture and give
And love like it's our soul's purpose

How we build each other back up
When a boy has torn us down

How we've claimed our stake
In every industry
While still birthing generations

How we can make men weak
Or build them powerful
By a simple look in our eyes

How we've taken this female body
Stubborn and needy
And turned it into a blessing

What a blessing to have come from you

Part 2: The Untangling

Pull

When they ask me why I love you
My mouth freezes in a wide grin

I could say
It feels like a deep sense of knowing
All the way down into my belly
Or as though there were a cord tied from my
chest to your fingertips

I could say
When I first saw you smile I thought I had
finally seen perfection
Or when I am with you both hands of the
clock stop moving
As if they too were dazzled by your allure

But none of this does it justice
No list of qualities
No string of words
Could explain the feelings you give me

And trying to explain it
Would be like trying to provide an
explanation
For why I am drawn to write
It simply calls to my soul

*How much harder loving anyone else has become
since I loved you*

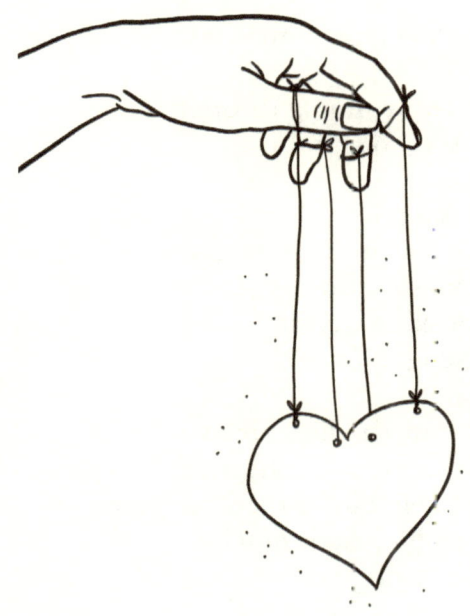

Utah

Our first flight together
The attendant must have felt our lust
She upgraded us to first class
Told us the next time she sees us
There better be a ring on my finger
And you promised her with a wink
Your charm never failing

We sipped on champagne
Till the plane landed in Utah
And we stepped out into a white wonderland

Boarded down the powdered trails of Park
City
Like two kids running through trees
Criss-crossing our tracks

I tried to keep up
But you were always so far ahead
The daredevil in you
Never scared of a crash
Always going full speed

I envied your childlike ability to play
To be so caught up in the moment
I couldn't help but be there with you
To stop my incessant thinking
To drop into my body
How you made me feel my body

I could have stayed there
With you
And the white shimmering trees
Till the snow caps melted
And the birds returned

Love

My world stops in your presence

How dangerous it is
To let go of everything else
In order to soak up more of you

Shooting Stars

You me and the vast open desert
Drunk off each other and red wine
Cheeks sore from laughing
Tongues sore from talking
Bodies sore from loving

But the clouds rolled in quickly
Not to worry
The neighbors assured us
The storm always passes us by
This spot is lucky

Not today

Our love so destructive it made the clouds
start a war
Hail hit the curved canvas walls of the yurt
Giant ice rocks pounding around us

But we loved the chaos
Both children of broken homes
Remember how our shouting words
Always turned into the sweetest love making

When the storm subsided
And the stars filled the sky
I made you come outside

It's freezing! You're nuts
You shouted
But I needed to see those sparkling lights
Dance across the sky
Needed to be reminded
How infinite this world is
How even if you leave again
Life will go on
In a million different possible ways
And besides
Aren't wishes worth freezing for?

Honey

I am deeper than any pot of honey
You've stuck your fingers into

But you don't know how to appreciate the
sweetness

Daisy

He loves me
He loves me not
He loves me
Called me this morning
Told me he can't wait to spend forever with
me
Asked me to dinner
Said he'd pick me up at five

Arrived eyes glossy
Five beers deep
Forgot the flowers he said he'd bring me
Loves me not

Cuddled me all night
Ran his fingers through my curly knots
Kissed every inch of my body
Loves me

Left abruptly the next morning
Told me he was busy
Didn't bother to make plans
Loves me not

Texted me *Good morning beautiful*
Can't wait to see your face
Loves me

Added five new chicks on socials
Said I shouldn't worry

Said he doesn't ask about my friends
      Why should I ask about his
Loves me not

Said we'll end up together
We're soulmates
Won't this make for a great love story

      Loves me?

Cheat

Did your eyes meet across a crowded room
Just like ours did
Did she make you laugh
Revealing your irresistible smile

Or was she mysterious
Soft spoken with dark eyes
Something the boy in you
Had to conquer
Even if it meant losing what you had

When you returned to me
Did any bit of guilt
Seep into your cold heart

Or did you feel giddy
For pulling off an untraceable crime
For conning a woman
As powerful as I

.

.

.

If our connection was as deep as you say
You would have felt my pain as yours
As you kissed her lips

(Empty) Words

I'm a sucker for words
Always have been
Naive to actions
Because I kneel to the spoken song

I will marry you one day
You said
I will get my shit together and make it right

One day
That was your answer
When I told you I needed space
Needed to think about allowing this pretty
poison back into my well

One day
As if I were a doll
Waiting patiently on a shelf
Once loved and adored
Now cast aside for newer toys
I know that game
I dropped my Cabbage Patch doll the second
holiday Barbie came out
Don't we all eat up novelty

One day
But these crumbs of lies
Can only sustain me for so long
I'm getting hungry for a man who means
what he says

.... One Day

He'll realize it
Momma said
One day
Didn't she know all too well
The price paid
When a man takes you for granted

One day
When you settle into yourself
The cravings for others will fade
The thirst for attention will no longer satiate
you
The thrill of the chase will become a tiring
burden
And you'll be left to fill the emptiness that
remains
By reaching inward
By pursuing meaningful ventures
By exploring your own soul
Rather than other people's bodies

Only then may you come to realize
How deep the love I had for you was
To endure the pain
Loving you brought with it

Bye/Hello

I've said *goodbye* to you
More times than I can count
      But you are still my favorite *hello*

Love Fern

You tell me I turn everything into a poem or
a metaphor
But that is how I see the world

Are you telling me it's a coincidence
That the pupils in our eyes widen in the
darkness
To allow more light to enter
Just as our hearts bleed open in pain
To allow more softness to grow within us

And that the death of my once full fern
Standing next to my bed frame
Losing nearly all of its foliage
Decided to begin completely anew
Sprouting new stems
Rather than repairing those he already had

Isn't he showing us
That sometimes the best choice
Is to start fresh
To allow what's withering
To die
And give space
For something better

Familiar

I wonder if they saw themselves
In each other's eyes
When they shook hands

Two men who knew all too well how to con a
woman
How to fall deep and fast
Only to run away with fear
Before making it to the finish line

Just don't hit her
Were my father's only words of advice
To the man who would end up breaking my
heart

Well he didn't hit me dad
Not to worry
There are no bruises on this pretty face
You call your child's
This pretty face
You saw too infrequently
This pretty face
You claim to know

The bruises he gave me
Were with hands that wanted nothing more
Than to please their owner
At the grasp of my curves
And the expense of my heart

The bruises he gave me
Were with a tongue that whispered lies
Using my dreams to get what he wanted

The bruises he gave me
Felt even more tender
Because it was a wound I already had

The bruises he gave me
Were now ones I could finally tend to
Because I felt their existence
Because I now knew where they laid

Incompatibility

How foolish was I anyhow
To think
I could fulfill his appetite for sex
And he
Feed my thirst for contemplation

Tee

I hate to admit
That your soft black tee is still my favorite
nightgown
Even though I promised I burnt all of the shit
you left behind
On a full moon filled with rage
In the firepit of the yard you once called
home

And I still can't go a day without picturing
your perfect smile
And allowing your face to dance across my
memory screen

And I hate that I swore you wouldn't get
another page of my journal
And yet here I am
Because you may quite possibly be my
favorite thing to write about
But you always made me break promises to
myself
      n o I can't tolerate that
But n o I can't leave

And I'm not sure what's a greater run on -
this poem or our broken love story -
And as I write this I'm beginning to realize
that it's me who doesn't want the story to end
That I am the one scared of closing the book
Because I'm terrified of the next chapter

Because the pain you've caused I've grown to
deal with
In fact
I've grown to use it as the fuel to my fire
And what will I do if it all burns out
And I'm left with a happiness I don't know
how to handle or a heart that's too mended
and too filled that it doesn't spill out onto
pages

Anxious

I fear
That my caring will always teeter the border
of smothering
That loving someone may always mean that
my mind runs crazy with the thought of
losing them
That my body will mistake unsafe and
uncertain for chemistry and butterflies
That my gut will tell me he's the one when he
is the one I should avoid
That real love will come knocking on my
doorstep and I'll turn it away because I don't
recognize it

I worry
That I don't know how to love properly
That since the moment I watched my father
pack his suitcase
I've been searching for a man who fits the
description of that red lipstick label

Fajitas

I chose for so long
To see the saint inside the sinner
To feed the light in you
Ignoring your shadows

Until I saw clearly
That night at dinner
When my eyes began to swell
And my voice tremble
At the lie I once again caught you in

And for the first time I realized
You could not console me
Didn't have the tools
You've never let your own heart feel that
deeply
How could you recognize my pain

You sat there eyeing your fajitas
Those shrimp sizzling
Hotter than the blood beginning to boil in my
veins
Can we eat now
You asked
As salty tears ran down my cheeks
Sure
I said
Eat up

And while you made your precious taco
I wiped the tears from my own face
This time I'll leave on my terms
I thought

I poured my tall glass of ice water
Into your skillet of prawns
Dousing the torch
That once kept me drawn to you
Left you alone at the table
To feast on your own bullshit

I blame the poet in me
For needing a dramatic ending

Heart

Today I went for a walk
And I plucked a white rose
For no reason
Twisting its sepal with my palm
As I pried it from its stem
Letting each petal fall to the sidewalk below
me
One
By
One
With each step I took
Until there was nothing left
But a carcass of once-beauty

Maybe I wanted to see how it felt
To destroy something beautiful
To have something delicate in my hands
And watch it fall apart

Did you feel that powerful too

(Not) One Night

Fireman mustache
And dark eyes to match
He walked right up to me
And asked me to dance
He hugged my hips
Thinking surely I'd take him home
And when I didn't
His words grew angry
Oh you're too old for fun
Too scared
That last man must have fucked you up

Maybe he did
In all the right ways
You see
He fucked the naivety right out of me
I see through those eyes of lust
And know they are ephemeral

I'm looking for eyes
That see me as magical
Something to be forever explored
Not hastily consumed in a night

I'd rather finish my evening alone
With a cigarette between my lips
And a pen in my hand
Than with a man between my thighs
Whose name I'll forget the next morning

Sacrifice

What you'll never know
Is that I made sure to wear your favorite
thong when I knew you'd see me naked that
evening
Even though I hated the way it pinched my
hips
And I cooked your favorite meal every time
you asked
When I couldn't care less for salmon and slaw
And what you didn't appreciate
Is that I sacrificed my own dreams
To try to fit you in my story
I wanted slow and you wanted fast
I wanted country and you beach city
Cast aside my passions
To ask *what do you want to do today baby*
When I should have taken that pen and
notepad outside
Laid in the grass
And let my heart guide me
Let it scream that I'm not listening
This is not how love should feel

But I didn't

So I'll now own every sacrifice
I'll take my love elsewhere
Just maybe not as fast as you did

You can tell the new hairstylist you're dating
That you like your shirts folded down the
sides
What a cute pairing you two make
Her fake blonde locks and your shiny bald
head
I bet your conversations are as deep as the
puddle of exhaust your beat up black Subaru
left on my driveway
Does she ask about your deepest fears or do
you love that it's kept light and fun
Something I tried so hard to be but I can't
ignore the thoughts that swirl in my mind

But I don't want to sound petty
I truly wish you two the best
Just know that when I say best
I mean what you deserve
I wish you what get what you deserve
And that may be pretty on the outside but we
know what your insides look like
The question is
Does she

Healing

When that plane lands
And my toes reach paradise
I will jump into that salt water
Let its abrasion
Rub off the scars you left on me

Lie in the sun and
Let it's warmth burn off every memory
My skin still holds of your kisses

Walk in the jungle
Until my mind forgets how to say your name
Because the trees have whispered
You are enough
You are worthy
And they look so damn beautiful
That I actually listen

Mountains

Mountains are formed
When two land masses collide
Shaking the foundation
Letting insides burst out
Warming the surroundings
And bleeding into one

Eventually when it cools
When the rumble subsides and the land is laid
to rest
Beauty quietly emerges
Coloring the surrounding landscape
In unique patterns of lines and edges
Calling in life
With the enchantment of trees

When the sky is clear
I can see each ridge
With beautiful dimensions
The shades of green and brown
Painted in the landscape

A reminder of
How beauty is birthed through pain
How growth is built by destruction
And love
Formed when souls collide

A reminder of you

Strength

I am grateful
for the strength I built from our

D

      E

S

      T

   R

U

     C

        T

I

       O

   N

Princess Bride

My father owned just one movie
Every other weekend when we'd visit as kids
We would rewatch the tape and
Listen to him quote
In an exaggerated Spanish accent
> *My name is Inigo Montoya*
> *You killed my father*
> *Prepare to die*

Revenge and power and adventure
What a story it was
But I know why he really loved it
Like all great stories it was more than a battle
of egos and swords
It was a story of love and sacrifice
Of how a man will fight monsters
Brave swamps and endure torture
To get the woman of his dreams
And ride off on white horses with her by his
side

That is how I know
That men who hold true love in their hands
only to squander it
Men who become all too familiar with
watching tears flow from their lover's eyes
Men who promise the world only to give small
pieces of themselves because they are terrified

of being caught in the shrapnel of a love too
explosive
Those men crave a fairytale too
Somewhere deep within them
Before their young selves felt the first fist of
heartache
Lies a boy who wants desperately
to whisper

As

    you

        wish

Accountability

I am the writer of my story
long before a pen is in my hand

Memories

I am keeping you alive in my thoughts
Scared to let you fade
Knowing soon you'll be nothing but a faint
image-

A representation of who I was then

Puzzles

This is the last poem you will get
Let me write that again so I believe it
THIS is the last poem you'll get
The last time my pen will spell your name
The last time words of you will grace my
pages
The last time I'll feed into the thoughts of our
past

But damn we had a good run
Less of a run
And more of a rollercoaster
I suppose
That's how it had to happen
Had to give us the jolt of adrenaline
We needed to beat that climb
To make it to the top of the mountain
And see every inch of our true selves

Remember when you couldn't sleep
Because we couldn't finish our thousand
piece puzzle
Before the dark of the night grew our eyes
heavy

You said the anxiety of those missing pieces
Kept your brain wired
You couldn't stop thinking about how each
rounded edge fit inside the next

I used to feel that same feeling
A deep feeling of incompleteness
How could we not make this work
When our bodies laid so perfectly together
Each curve of mine firmly against yours

Now I've slowly come to accept
That your face will always make me smile
Your body always make me weak
But this puzzle was never meant to be solved
  Together

You see
I played into your games
I ate up your lies
Because it was a feast that tasted familiar
Like the red sauce on my grandma's
meatballs
You reminded me of home
But as my pen gets tired and my heart slowly
begins to heal
I am learning
That not all stories must be rewritten
They just must come to an end

Meatballs Pt. 2

I want a family of my own and a man who
doesn't leave and a child with curls that
reminds me of my mother's and mine
before I damaged them with hot irons and
expectations. And she smiles when I ask her
if she wants to make meatballs and as we're
grating the parmesan her dad is outside the
window tending to the garden and his skin is
glowing in the last hour of sunlight and I think
how lucky I am to have written this new story.

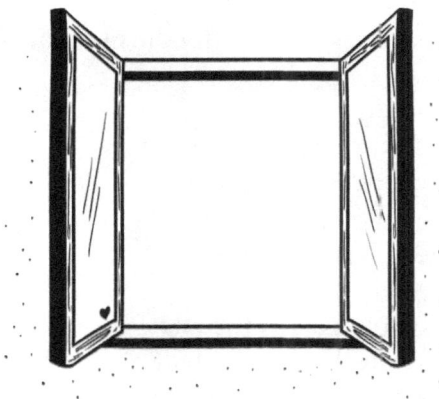

Moon

I see the moon and the moon sees me
And the moon sees the somebody I want to see
God bless the moon and god bless me
And god bless the somebody I want to see

My mother used to sing that rhyme to us as
kids
Every night the moon lit up the sky
It's fullness a reminder
Of how small this world is
How even if another soul seems too far away
to feel
In distance or in heart
We are all under the same stars
Our hands never too far apart

The other night as I read
Tucked cozily in my bed
Under the blanket of the sky
I came across the second half of the rhyme
That I never knew existed

I sent it to my mother
It reads
If I get to heaven before you do
I'll make a hole and pull you through
I'll write your name on every star
And that way the world won't seem so far

Have you heard that part of the rhyme before?
I asked her
No
She replied
but I love it

.

.

.

Isn't that what children are for
To take what is given and expand it
To carry on the song

Love Poem

If I could go back to my younger self
Before I felt the first ounce of unworthiness
Before I experienced true heartbreak
Before I learned the darkness that exists
Both in the world
And inside of me
Here is what I'd say:

There is such little in life we have control over
Such little worth fretting over
Take it as it comes
All of it impermanent

Fully embrace the moments of joy
However small
The ones that make you grin
Exposing your teeth to the wind
Etching wrinkles near your eyes

And stay present in the times that are testing
Those that make your stomach sew knots
And eyes swell with tears

Avoid escaping the body with booze
Or filling the mind with distractions
Sit with it
Learn from it
Face it
It's not that scary
It's simply life saying

Here I am
In all my glory
Beautiful and ugly
Warm and harsh
Tender and painful
And in this duality
This constant ride
Can you find peace
A home within yourself
Untied to the outcome
Simply in awe of the journey

.
.

You are born with everything you need
Remember that
Place your hand on your beating heart
This is your home
And it will always be there
Waiting for your arrival
After exploring the world
Eager to welcome you back
No questions asked

Spare yourself the judgment
Careful not to feed the nagging critic that will
undoubtedly develop in your mind
Learn to laugh at her thoughts
Embrace her presence like a protective friend

As you grow you'll gain wisdom through
experience
You'll be both the victim and the villain
Because both parts must be played to fully
write your story

You'll laugh and love and be in joy
In so many different ways and with so many
different people
But you'll also experience pain and sadness
Loss and regret
Heartache and heartbreak
You'll grow from these too

So lean in
Feel it all
Don't be scared
Place your hand on your chest again
It's still beating
You're still there

If someone isn't treating you right
No matter how much you love them
I hope you have the courage to walk away
Because you remember
Your first love is yourself

If something is wrong
I hope you speak up
And declare your truth
Even if there are consequences

Because these moments
Will help define who you are
They will give power to your voice
Building bricks for you to stand tall on
If you forget your own strength
Go outside and look up at the stars
Remember you are birthed from their
explosion
That fire within you can never be put out

When things don't go your way
When every door seems to close
When someone you love exits your story
When you begin to lose hope in that fairytale
ending
Remember the point of this crazy beautiful
experience
Is to simply enjoy it
To know your soul better
To shed every layer
Helping to bring you closer home
To that bright beating heart
To love

CREDITS

"Moon" was inspired after reading Sarah Kay's poem *Astronaut* – which provided the second part of the nursery rhyme (from her collection *No Matter the Wreckage* (2014))

"The Princess Bride" was written after the amazing classic film *The Princess Bride* (1987)

ACKNOWLEDGEMENTS

My Mother: You love more fiercely and passionately than anyone I have ever encountered. Thank you for showing me how to be a strong woman who is not afraid to use her voice. And thank you for being so patient with the time it took for me to discover my own.

My Father: Your role in this narrative is only a sliver of the story of our lives. Thank you for showing me that men do indeed reflect and grow. I love you always.

My Stepfather: I've felt you every step of this writing journey. There are no words I can write which you haven't already felt.

My Sister: Thank you for helping to edit this work even if the words I spoke of the child version of you were harsh. I cannot imagine my life without a sister, and I'm honored to call you mine.

Thank *you* for joining me on this journey.

With love,

Tracy

ABOUT THE AUTHOR

Tracy lives in Southern California.

WORKS BY THIS AUTHOR

Contemplations:
A collection of poetry & prose

Lessons from our Animal Friends:
A children's interactive picture book